Should I
Tell Them the
Truth
or Let Them
Keep Believing a Lie?

CAROL BLACKWELL

ISBN 979-8-88685-841-9 (paperback)
ISBN 979-8-88685-842-6 (digital)

Christian Faith Publishing
832 Park Avenue
Meadville, PA 16335
www.christianfaithpublishing.com

Printed in the United States of America

I have been accused of being too blatant with the tongue.
My belief is if asked a question, one probably wants a truthful
answer. We cannot make proper judgments if we do
not have the whole truth. It may hurt or make you mad even,
but the bottom line…now we know.

The most dangerous liars are those who
think they are telling the truth.

—Themindjournal.com

CONTENTS

ACKNOWLEDGMENTS

All glory and praise belong to God the Father, Jesus Christ the Son, and the Holy Spirit. Without You, I could not have overcome what I overcame. I am deeply grateful for Your guidance and Your faithfulness.

Darryl G. Blackwell, the best husband and friend I could hope for. You have been the greatest example of how a man is to love his wife. Every time I think about how the Lord brought us together, I am filled with gratitude.

To my precious sisters, Christine and Faye, who encouraged me in every way to write this story, listened as I read what I had written along the way, and gave wonderful suggestions to how to say it better. Thank you!

My friend Martha Jones, it was because of your courage that I found mine. You are special.

There were those of you who prayed and prophesied the Word of God over this project. Thank you for your love!

CHAPTER 1

The Question

Therefore, rejecting all falsehood [whether lying, defrauding, telling half-truths, spreading rumors, any such as these], speak truth each one with his neighbor, for we are all parts of one another [and we are all parts of the body of Christ].

—Ephesians 4:25 AMP

I was struggling with this one question: *Should I tell them the truth, or let them keep believing a lie?*

The summers were always nice, and the streets were often filled with people driving by in their cars with windows down; bicycles zooming by, and the corner store bustled with boys hanging in the front having fun. Back then there was no need for seat belts or helmets for your bike. It wasn't the law. Some days the summer heat was just enough that if you had air-conditioning in the car, you didn't need to turn it on. We would much rather have the windows down to holler with a "Glad to see ya" at people we knew…or didn't know. But my thing was walking. Only because Daddy hadn't bought my car yet.

It was a good day to wear my orange jumpsuit and a sleeveless top underneath as I walked. There was a blue car that was riding up and down this long stretch of road with this same bozo-looking head driving. Each time I saw this car, the man would beep his horn at me.

At seventeen years old this was a big deal. A man thought I was cute enough to beep the horn at. Wowee doggie!

Coming home from school one day, guess what was parked across the street? Yes, indeed, that blue car. I believe I sat on the front stoop until the bozo head came out of the house. He spoke to me! I acted like "hi" very low key. I forgot to say how shy I was back then. Shy in my own way. Somehow, we struck up some kind of conversation, and I was so very captivated. This was an older, smooth-talking somebody with a car, and he was flirting with me. The car showed up across the street more often. Well, his mom lived there. She was a nice, kind of strange holy woman. I didn't understand that stuff.

As we continued talking, my mother noticed me keeping company with Bozo Head…wait… I should call him a name. Let's go with Leon. Momma said, "Carolann, you don't need to be talking to that man!"

"Why, Momma?" Remember I am an impressionable seventeen-year-old.

"Because that man is married!"

"No, he ain't, Momma. He's separated!" Good grief, how dumb do they come! I was green. Fresh-off-the-*Mayflower* green. Of course, I wasn't going to listen to her. She didn't know anything. Besides, Leon loved me. He told me that when we snuck in his momma's house to go upstairs while she was asleep, then we snuck back out. I was seventeen; he was old. He got comfortable taking me around his family, his sisters especially. There were a lot of them.

One day we rode over to Leon's sister's house, two of his sisters were there. I was so sleepy. Linda told me to go lie down on the bed in her room. I did. On the way I heard her say, "I think she's pregnant." I paid it no attention, but in the back of my mind I was screaming *Nooooooo!* But as it turns out, I was. By this time, I had been eighteen for a while.

I want to say something about my mother right now. She worked hard as a beautician, worked diligently studying to be a nurse, and worked many hours a day being a nurse at Dixie Hospital. She did the best she could as far as being there for me and my sisters to guide and teach us something about life. It was surely up to me to listen. I didn't. After all, in my eyes she was too old to know anything about today's happenings in the world. That being said, our relationship was mostly strained because of what I believed she failed to do for me as a young kid. That, I will talk about later. Anyway, Momma would have dreams about us. Guess what she dreamed about me? You got it! I was pregnant. When she told me her dream, I could do nothing but hold my head down and say yes. I was embarrassed and ashamed that I did not heed her advice and leave that man alone. Momma did not put me out, did not scold me too badly, but she supported and helped me like she loved me. She did. And I loved her. The relationship was still strained though. The way I saw it, I was a sinner. My mother and the two sisters I grew up with were sinners too. We loved sin. That's what we knew, so that's what we did. But there is a consequence. I got pregnant.

At eighteen years old, I graduated from high school with hopes of becoming a social studies teacher. I loved social studies and my teacher, Mr. Baker, was such a great instructor. I remember asking him where he went to school because that seemed to be the place to go for such learning. I asked him if I could still go if I'm pregnant. *Still green, y'all.* I only remember the disappointment in his face when I said that. That look caused me to think that there was no hope. It was the end for me. I could never fulfill life dreams that I had. Life was over. I was having a baby. Funny thing, no one ever talked to me about going to school, and I was pretty smart book-wise.

Okay, back to Bozo Head… I mean Leon. My mom had words with him. (*Sorry, can't write them here. She was not in the Lord at the time and had much liberty to speak as a sinner would express expletives.*) She wanted to have him arrested for statutory rape. Because I was a little dense back then and foggy in the head, I believe I asked her not to, *or* she did not because I was eighteen. She did not realize that the relationship started when I was seventeen. Wow, he dodged a bullet, Bozo Head. *Now* I don't want to have anything to do with him. And I didn't. He wanted to be in the baby's life. He asked to come see him and buy him things. I did not allow him to. I didn't know what I was doing. Emotions were all over the creation. My old boyfriend was back in my life now, in the middle of all this confusion. We decided to get married before the baby was born, and this caring man gave the baby his name as if he was the biological father. How ironic that the biological father and my new husband had the same last name. No relation.

Mom had prepared for the wedding that I was not sure at all I wanted to happen as the date drew nearer. My sister told me that I was walking around like a zombie. I was disconnected. Momma did not have much to invest in a big wedding, but she did have a lot of favor and friends. The day was approaching quickly, and my decision was certain… I did not want to get married. Fear gripped me fiercely, and I could not bring myself to tell Momma that I did not want to get married. She had spent so much effort and money pulling things together. I went through with it. Bad choice. Nice man in the beginning, but bad choice to be married. Anyway, we lived together for three long years. It was three long years of other people all in the middle of our marriage. I'll say it again, bad choice. And by the way, the older people at the wedding reception behaved like it was the party of the century. I have pictures to prove it!

It's hard for me to understand why no one was talking to me about things that I thought somebody should have been talking to me about. Like, labor hurts!

My husband was in the US Army boot camp. I lived with mom at the time in a two-bedroom apartment with my sisters. Oh my goodness, can I tell you some stories about my sisters! Momma was still working at the hospital and naturally had friends and coworkers that she had bonded with. When I started having pain, I was so nervous and scared, not knowing if I was going to lose a body part or not! She took me to the hospital, they rolled me in, laid me on a bed, checked out my bottom, and said, "Not quite ready yet."

What! I hurt—I hurt bad. The pain went away. It is called *contractions*. In other words, the baby was giving me very hard spasms. This back and forth went on for a while. You all know that they put a hospital gown on you with the opening in the back, right? Okay. This is what happened. Momma went to get something to eat and drink. On her way back from a good distance down the hall she could hear me screaming these words: "*Momma, Momma, Momma!*"

She did not know what in the world was happening. The sound was earsplitting. She runs into the room and sees nothing but my behind in the air, as I had turned over trying to alleviate the excruciating spasms. The doctor and nurse were going to give me something for the pain, but by the time they were going to administer it, I had knocked myself out, had the baby, and morning had come. I opened my eyes to a brand-new day, but my stomach was still huge. I asked the attending nurse, "Did I have the baby yet?"

She gave me one of those "Are you insane?" looks and said yes.

"What did I have?"

Again, with the look. "A boy."

"Okay."

She brought the baby in, laid him on my chest, and I'm thinking, what am I supposed to do now? I looked at him. He was the most precious, chubby-cheeked baby boy I had ever seen. I loved him!

When Momma would tell the story about November 19, 1974, she reminds me that I embarrassed her in front of her friends and coworkers. Oh well, nobody told me about the excruciating pain; do you think that I may have been a bit more prepared if I knew what was coming? I got to find out two and a half years later.

As years rolled on, the blue car was still coming across the street. Momma no longer lived on the street, of course, but my grandparents did. Granddaddy would have my son all the time. They were like two peas in a pod. But the chubby-cheeked boy still did not know who his biological father was, and I did not tell him until he was eight years old, because I had to.

My husband and I were not together anymore. We were not really ready for marriage. We tried. In those three years I was led to Jesus by my mother. She got saved and shared with me and my sisters her newfound life in God. The transformation was unbelievable. You had to know my mom to know that this was a *sho nuff* miracle! In 1975 I was born again. Bless the Lord!

I joined the church where Mom was, and every service was taking me deeper into the things of God as I learned and listened and trusted. One thing that had not changed was the fact that I was still green. I thought everybody in the church was saved and loved Jesus. There was a woman named Fannie that I had connected with after being in this church for six years. We became friends. I needed a saved friend with whom I could be comfortable expressing my thoughts and feelings about things that were personal to me. I loved her because she listened to me and seemed to genuinely care. Fannie didn't drive, so I would pick her up for church, but mostly she would only need a ride home after a service. I get overemotional sometimes. I wanted to share some of my life's overcoming moments with her, and I told her about my son and his father. After I finished, it seemed like she was trying not to rush me out of her house, but she did in a subtle way. That was the last time she talked to me as a friend. I felt rejected and betrayed. This is what transpired in a very short time.

CHAPTER 2

I'm Out!

Before I knowed it, I was saying out loud, "The hell with it!
There ain't no sin and there ain't no virtue. There's
just stuff people do. It's all part of the same thing. And some
of the thing's folks do is nice, and some ain't nice,
but that's as far as any man got a right to say."

—John Steinbeck, *The Grapes of Wrath*

I had no idea that Bozo Head's wife and family were members of the church. Now that I think about it, seemed like everybody was related to somebody somehow. Anyway, Fannie told the family; and thus, my life was forever changed again.

At that time the church owned a nice restaurant serving great food. I was a waitress. Everyone was sitting at the bar talking. They looked at the door, saw me, and stopped talking. Quiet. It felt really weird, and I wanted to run out. Instead, I spoke and kept it moving. It was the heaviest day of work ever. The manager called me to a meeting. He was a minister at the church as well.

"Sis, just do one thing. Don't leave the church."

"I don't know what I'm going to do. This is hard. What did I do wrong?"

"Just hold on. Don't leave."

How can you work with people who aren't talking to you and don't even want you around? I left the job. It didn't bring any peace, but at least I didn't have to face the ugliness coming from the *tearing-up-the-aisle-dancing, hollering-all-over-the-place-how-good-God-is Christians.* They treated me horribly. There were one or two sane ones, but they were caught between loyalty to the family and the outsider. I cried a lot. What had I done wrong?

In hindsight, I should have had a long conversation with the bishop of the church. Others were talking to him and lying to him. He did ask me what I told Fannie. I told him. He asked, "Why did you tell her?"

"I thought she was my friend, and that I could trust her."

That was that. I saw no need to talk to him anymore about it because I had been under his tutelage for six years; surely, he knew my character. The things that they were saying would have never been seen or said of me. Certainly, he would know that. He believed the lies. The bishop actually believed the lies. I had no defense. I knew what was being said because the family had a mole in the camp.

They said, "She came in here [work] talking about 'I don't care what they say, my baby gonna see his daddy!'" I never said anything like that. The mole had revealed that someone was asked to beat me up. This is coming from the people I thought were saved.

There was a convocation of some sort happening this same week. There were people from all over the state attending all week. I enjoyed the excitement as the saints came together to praise and worship the Lord. It helped me to cope. I didn't talk to anybody during this season, just came to church. For one thing, I felt alone. The two church sisters that I had allowed to live in my house stayed away from me. My mom and my blood sisters didn't really say much. It was like they all believed I had done wrong. Because Bishop believed them, the verdict was in. I was guilty. Because Bishop believed them.

Flashback... There was a song by Luther Ingram back during the really green and dumb-de-dumb-dumb days—"If Loving You is Wrong, I Don't Wanna Be Right." You know what? I hate that song! That song was my truth in 1973–74. My truth stunk! A wrong was committed. Sin had reigned. That song was playing when Leon's sister was over my mom's with me. I was singing it like I had written the godforsaken lyrics. Then I wondered, *Why is she looking at me so strange?*

I had a baby by a married man. When I was a sinner, I was sinning. That is what real sinners do. That is as real as it gets, I suppose. I was definitely a real sinner.

I want to go back to why I didn't think too much about talking to the bishop about what was going on. It was my understanding that when you give your life to God, every sin is forgiven; it's under the blood of Jesus; it's done, thrown in the sea of forgetfulness where He remembers them no more. So it will turn out just fine, I thought. I reckon God forgot to tell these people that. *No*, He didn't. We should never forget what the grace and mercy of God has done in our lives when we are tempted to condemn another.

There is now no condemnation to those who are in Christ Jesus! Okay. I am in Christ Jesus, washed clean by His precious and life-giving blood. *(I'm sorry, I think I got off course, let me find my way back to the convocation…)*

Tuesday night of the convocation, Bishop was up talking about something, then he shifted and was talking about me and my sin. I shut down, and all I heard was, "She can't testify in this church for six months, and she has to go before the Mother's Board." What did he just say? It was like being in bizarro world! Do you understand how it feels to want to cry, but refuse to cry? Your feet are telling you to storm out, but you sit in bewilderment? What just happened in front of all these people? I felt like two cent waiting for change. That was the last night I ever set foot in that church. I was not welcomed, I was not appreciated, I was an outcast. Oh well, if the church didn't want me, I knew who did. The Silver Dollar Club and Restaurant! Off we go!

This is a new kind of pain for me. This is one of the greatest examples of "church hurt," and I didn't even know then what church hurt was. To be enamored with anybody and placing them on an undeserved pedestal is dangerous to both parties. I'm so sure that I was not the only one who was hurt in this thing. When you hurt badly, sometimes it's hard to think about somebody else's pain. But I did.

I cannot begin to tell you how determined I was to never step foot in this church or any other church again. Ever. Never. I'm done! Momma and my little sister would make it their business to come by the house to get me back in the church, or give me Jesus talk, and we cannot forget about the threatening, "Carolann, if you don't come back, you're going to hell."

My response to that, "Well, I'll be happy on my way!" To even think those words came out of my mouth makes me shudder to this very day!

CHAPTER 3

Tip

*Tip: If you are going to sin, get it right the first time. You may
not have a second chance to sin that way again like I did.*

Who goes from attending church almost every night of the
week, to clubbing at least three times a week? I do, I do! And
boy was I having a slamming, good old time. The Silver Dollar was
my new church. The bartender was the pastor, the DJ was the praise
and worship team, the waiters and waitresses were the deacons of the
church. As normal, there were more women than men at my new
church. Thursday night garnered just as many or more congregants
than Saturday or Sunday. I believed that I was on my way to hell, so
I may as well enjoy the go. That was a two-year run. After that everything started to go downhill. Oh well.

***Station Break: My first time backsliding
after two years saved***

The Bible says that the joy of sin lasts a season. Seasons come,
and seasons go. This reminds me of a time when I decided to backslide. I must have backslid twice because this was a different season.
Oh yeah, I remember why I started sinning this time. Not telling
you though. The Langley NCO Club was open on Sundays, and I
went to dance my dance and drink my daddy's drink, Bourbon and

11

Coke and smoke my grandmother's Salem cigarettes. Sitting in the seat looking cool, jazzy and with it, everything started looking hazy red. It was rather frightening. I heard a voice in my head say, "You're going to hell with the rest of them." How many of you know that was the last time I went to the Langley Air Force Base NCO Club! To go a little further in my backsliding right after the NCO Club warning, I went to some club across the Chesapeake Bay. It was rather ritzy. Since I was new at this backsliding thing, I did not have backslider nightclub clothes, I had serious sanctified church clothes on at the club, y'all! This is funny because I couldn't respond properly to a sinner joke with my church girl clothes on without saying "Hallelujah!" *Awkward*. Yes, I got the looks. So out of place. *And* I couldn't do the hustle dance everybody was doing. One guy felt sorry for me, I guess, and offered to teach me. Maybe he couldn't get anybody else to dance with. It was a flop. As hard as I tried, I couldn't make a very good backslider. If you're going to sin you should do it right.

Continuing my second backslide

There was a friend of Mom's who allowed me to live with her family in the eleventh grade, Miss Grafton. She gave me a good home along with her husband, son, and daughter. As I was going through my backsliding days, I called her one night because loneliness and depression was starting to set in. She was always good at talking me back to a place where I wouldn't snuff my own life. This good-hearted woman told me that I needed a man and a good bottle of something to drink. Hey! Let's do it! I got the bottle, but the man part was a bit of a challenge. What man? I started thinking about one or two that I had liked in school. I called Ronald. He came over. We talked. Only talked. He went home. He could have taken advantage of me, but he showed himself to be a real friend. He went home. I still had the bottle. From this point, being an old-fashioned alcoholic may not be such a bad idea. One problem. Where is the money for the firewater coming from? That plan went belly-up!

The Silver Dollar was my go-to place. Since Granddaddy didn't mind keeping the kids, I didn't mind asking him. The downward spiral of immoral living was starting to get darker, and it was as if I was no longer in control of my own life. Something inside of me was keeping me from going off the deep end though. Is this what depression feels like? I could see all of this movement around me. People laughing, drinking, smoking, dancing, having a good time. But it all seemed unreal to me now. I was lost. I felt trapped, and there was no one to come and rescue me. Where in hell am I? The advice from the well-meaning, good-hearted woman had taken me to another level of darkness.

I went home and stayed there. Literally. In my mind I was still going to hell, but it wasn't so happy anymore. Just numbness and hanging in limbo waiting to see what's going to happen next in this pitiful, dull so-called existence. Good grief, I was really depressed. I kept the kids and the apartment clean. We had food that I cannot remember how we got because I didn't go out. I do remember Granddaddy bringing bags of food sometimes. He knew something was going on with me but never addressed anything. He supported us as best as he knew how. Granddaddy had always been in my corner.

Can I take a break here and tell you a little about Granddaddy?

They called him "Scotty." A former drinker, always a pipe smoker, he loved children and loved his family. Scotty worked hard taking care of family. Momma sent me to my grandparents' house most of my childhood. I loved it there because Granddaddy spoiled me. He loved to see me eat, and I loved to eat! One day I fell down and skinned my knee. He was sitting on the porch in the rocking chair, smoking and holding his pipe. I can almost see him now. Always the same position. I came crying to the steps…

"What's the matter with you, child?"

"I fell and hurt my knee. It's got blood on it. Waa waa!"

"Fall down and skin the other one, then you will have a match."
I know that sounds mean, but that was his way of getting me to stop crying, and it worked. I don't know if I was in shock or if it was just funny. I walked away and finished playing. Granddaddy had a very

compassionate heart, said few words, but you could feel him. This old man was one whom I knew I could depend on.

It was good for me that Granddaddy didn't ask questions or make judgments about me. That would have taken me out for sure. My ex-husband's mom was a precious woman who looked out for us too. I will never forget her kindness to me. She made sure we had chicken. I wonder if this is one of the reasons that chicken is my favorite meat today. Hmmm? The good ole Baptist barnyard bird! Whether it is fried, baked, stir-fried, roasted, sliced, diced, broiled or boiled, you name it, I love chicken! I digress again…sorry. I'm depressed! I mean I'm depressed.

This went on for two years. Nighttime was the right time to get the mail and to walk across the street to the store for a pack of Kool Lights cigarettes. The only daylight my children saw was through the window or if Granddaddy came to get them. All three of us were looking right pale. Wow, what a nonlife.

If you will hang in there a little while longer, I'm getting ready to tell you about the good part now. *Hang in there with me, y'all!*

CHAPTER 4

The Strong Comeback after the First Backslide

This backsliding dilemma? It gets to be very wearisome when all of the joy is sucked clean out of it. So the thrill was over. God in His endless mercy welcomed me back into the fellowship of believers and put me straight to work. He never ever gave up on me, neither did He leave me. The following is what my week looked like when I returned to the church:

This is a rigid and tough schedule: Up at 3:30 a.m. to get the children and myself ready for 5:00 a.m. prayer and after prayer help cook breakfast for those who came to pray. Serving with the hospital ministry lead by one of the elders was a joy to me and scary all at the same time. The elder always gave an altar call after the message and offered to pray for those who wanted prayer. This one Sunday, he told me that I would be doing that. I was shaking all over. I've never done anything like this, but he had taught me well. I trusted God, and I trusted the man of God's example. I paid attention to all that he did. An older woman was helped to walk up to the front for prayer for her stomach. She looked about seven or eight months pregnant, but that was not her problem. I laid hands on her belly, and as we were praying, her stomach was going down under my hand! I'm putting a great big *hallelujah* right here! I learned *so* much. The elder was a wonderful teacher by words and example. Then back to the church house for Sunday school followed by church service all of Sunday up until eleven or twelve o'clock at night or longer, while the children were sleeping under the pews.

But Wait, There's More!

Monday through Friday or Tuesday and Friday noonday prayer. Monday night tarrying service. Oh, Monday night tarrying service. I wanted the Holy Ghost! Sometimes we were in the sanctuary and on other Mondays we were in the Sunday school room. Mother Blanchard would clear the floor of tables and chairs in this room, so I thought that I was supposed to roll on the floor to be baptized in the Holy Ghost; therefore, I rolled on the floor. No Holy Ghost. I would return the next Monday, and it went about the same. One night she decided to explain some things. Right there I felt so dumb. I didn't have to roll on the floor. I rolled on the floor for nothing. That is so funny to me now! I was a Holy Roller for real! We had Tuesday night service and of course Friday night is family night service. I almost forgot on Saturday we were across the water witnessing and asking for money for the television ministry. At one point I sang with the radio broadcast ensemble. That was when I had no car, so I walked with my son for forty-five minutes to an hour one way. I was not offered a ride. And it was okay. I didn't ask either, I don't think. Anyway!

Almost to the Excitement!

On the weekend when the liquor store would be booming with business, we'd be out in front standing on either side of the door with a container of some sort to put the donation money in. You are talking about one bold and fearless people. The men who came in and out of the ABC store gave. Sometimes they even hung around to hear about Jesus. That was the goal, you know. I also sang in the choir, so somewhere on this schedule there was choir rehearsal.

One thing I did learn about the God of heaven and earth, He has unconditional, genuine love for me…and you too. Yet I found a reason to backslide.

God said, "Return, O backsliding children, saith Jehovah; for I am a husband unto you: and I will take you one of a city, and two of a family, and I will bring you to Zion."

Just think, God said that before I was even thought about thousands of years down the road.

And here I am in this two-bedroom apartment down in the deepest of dumps.

Remember the first backsliding I told you I wasn't going to tell you about? This is the ending of that first season of backsliding I mentioned in chapter 3, second paragraph. (No, I am still not going to tell the reason why I did. It's more than I can bear.)

Something was different about this Tuesday morning. Granddaddy had come by and carried the chubby cheek boy with him. The baby was in the house somewhere. He was a good baby. Cute as a button. I was at the kitchen sink washing the same old raggedy dishes. I heard something in my head say to me, "Go pray."

"Go pray? I'll go pray when I finish washing dishes."

"Go pray now."

Without another word, I put the dish down, picked up the little one, and we both went in his room. I placed him on the floor with some toys. I backed away from him, lifted my hands in the air. Before I could start a prayer, a praise came out of my mouth, floods of tears rolled down my face. No one will ever believe this part right here… I looked down at my feet because they felt like they were no longer on the floor. They were not! I praised louder, "*Hallelujah, hallelujah, hallelujah!*" Running was in my feet. I ran from one room to the other, up and down the hallway, and back again. This running episode continued for a good while it seemed. Running and hallelujahs all over the apartment.

Because my little sister and Mom were so diligent in praying for me, I called Mom first to tell her that I had been touched by the Lord. When she answered the phone, nothing would come out of my mouth but Praise to God—*hallelujah!*

It felt like *hallelujah* was in the depths of my being pumping through my blood and forming the only praise to God that mattered at the moment. I was in a zone that I had never experienced in my entire life.

It seemed that the praise-a-thon was dying down now. I knew that there were three other people that I needed to call. Dialing my sister in law's number brought a whole new batch of praise. When she picked up the phone all she heard was *hallelujah, hallelujah, hallelujah!* "Who is this?" "Carol, *hallelujah!*" "I can't talk now, *hallelujah!*" I hang up the phone and proceed to run through the apartment again. Calmed again, I go in to get the baby to play with him. I'm on the bed tossing him up in the air and talking baby talk, when all of a sudden it wasn't baby talk anymore. I was speaking in tongues! *I got the Holy Ghost!* That's when I called the bishop's wife to tell her that I had the Holy Ghost. "I'm going to talk like I got the Holy Ghost, I'm going to walk like I got the Holy Ghost, and I'm going to act like I got the Holy Ghost!"

She says, "No, you let Him do the acting."

"Okay. Thank you." We hang up. What a refreshing time early Tuesday morning.

On my last birthday Li'l Sis had given me a cross necklace that just stayed on my dresser because I was not going to wear anything that looked like church. That Tuesday afternoon, I proudly put the most beautiful necklace on with a smile. Redemption had visited me. It's Tuesday. Oh wow, it's Tuesday! Church service is on Tuesday! Oh boy! I called Li'l Sis to tell her to pick me up for church, and please don't be late. She was late. I was crying because I thought that I was going to miss testimony service. She was late. We got there in time.

If you aren't Johnny-on-the-spot when it comes to testimony time in this church, you will miss out. You have to be like popcorn, or you may miss an opportunity to spill the praise about what God has done in and for you. This was my dilemma. There is one sister that you want to make sure you pop up before she does. She has a never-ending story to tell every single testimony time. It's good, but still long! We were running out of time and almost ready to move to the next portion of worship. I was praying inside, "Lord, am I going to have a chance? I've got to tell what You did. Please let me have a chance."

She sat down, I hurried and popped straight up. Then I couldn't say anything. Did I tell you that I was a little shy in those days? I was a little shy in those days. All I was doing was jerking from side to side. That was new. Then I opened my mouth. Out comes this voice I had not heard before. It was bold, it was strong, it was confident, and it was loud. Telling the story of my morning in demonstration, I moved out of the pew and walked down the aisle, not noticing eyes, voices, nothing. It was cloudy in the room; I saw no man. I walked back and forth at the altar talking and praising. When I was on my way back to my seat, it felt like my feet were not on the ground, same as it was in the apartment. This time I did not check. I just went with it. Oh my goodness, it was totally awesome the transformation that can take place in a dingy, dirty wretched soul! One visit from the Holy One changed my life…again.

Okay. So the next service we had, there was no shame in my standing up for testimony. I had the Holy Ghost. I was speaking about how good God has been to me and all of a sudden, the English changed to an unknown tongue. Beats me what it was. I just flowed with it. It was so smooth and precise. At that time, I was not educated on the gifts of the Spirit and how they flow. There should have been an interpretation given by one who had the gift of interpretation or according to the Bible, I should have given it. Didn't know. The moment I was coming down from that mount, Bishop walked in the room. When he got settled in the pulpit, he says, "Y'all better be careful of these tongues you're speaking."

Uh-oh. Did I have the Holy Ghost, or had I been possessed by a demon? I heard the Holy Ghost say, "Pay that no mind." I didn't. I knew what had happened in me. He was not there. I trusted this man of God, truly. But this time, Man of God, you missed the mark. It can happen to any human being.

CHAPTER 5

Almost Finished!

You have been given testimony on two consecutive backslidings that seemed to be so close that the antics were easy to get entangled into each other. But come on now, you know that is what sin does! It's confusing! These discombobulating backslidings, which led to the final dark side of living without any regard to what Jesus had done on the cross for me just about killed me.

You know what, dear reader? We have somehow put leaders on a pedestal that was not intended to be. Why did pastors and all those with authority allow us to do that? Why didn't we stop when it became evident that some of them had gotten too high and mighty, taking glory from God? How many of us still have the mindset that because the pastor said it, the bishop said it, the prophet said it, the teacher said it, that it must be the absolute truth? Not so. We are admonished to check the Word of God for ourselves. Yes, God has given us these precious ministry gifts in the body of Christ to help us grow, to edify us, and encourage us along the way. Ephesians 4:11 tells us this. But the bottom line: we must work out our own soul salvation with fear and trembling. This is what I read in Philippians 2:12 in the Amplified Bible…

> So then, my dear ones, just as you have
> always obeyed [my instructions with enthusiasm],
> not only in my presence, but now much more in

my absence, continue to work out your salvation
[that is, cultivate it, bring it to full effect, actively
pursue spiritual maturity] with awe-inspired fear
and trembling [using serious caution and criti-
cal self-evaluation to avoid anything that might
offend God or discredit the name of Christ].

I have now learned to hear what the Lord is teaching through His servant without lifting him or her to an exalted position where they do not belong. They are our brothers and sisters with a calling to do what God requires of them, as do you and I. That revelation took a minute to get because everybody and their momma was on the verge of making that leader a bona fide idol. Can't do that. God does not like it. Be humble. Everybody.

Two major backslidings. Wow. How does the Lord even have any dealings with us? Saved one day, a heathen the next. Or as the old folk used to say, "I laid my religion on the shelf, did what I was gonna do, and picked it back up."

Let's go back and deal with the second backsliding that sent me to the Silver Dollar, into depression, into promiscuity, into a second marriage, into partying hardily, into not really giving a hoot about life—at least mine anyway. Did I mention that I was smoking a pack and a half of cigarettes a day? Foolishness, a bunch of foolishness I tell you! Nobody understood. I didn't understand. But God did. Really though, where was all of this coming from? It could not have been because the saints lied about me to the bishop. I forgave them because they knew not what they were doing…maybe they did. Nonetheless, I forgave 'em. That was a humongous pill to swallow for them. I had a hard time forgiving my leaders though. I must tell you about how God brought me to the place of knowing I had forgiven.

I was doing just fine after my Pentecostal experience on that Tuesday morning. I loved church, y'all! These were the boldest days of my life. Church was my life. I wanted to please the Lord with everything I had. I wanted to work for God. So I took to the streets by myself. In the indigent part of the city where there was high crime, that is where I went. Jesus and I knocking on doors asking people if they knew Him, are you saved, would you like to be saved. And if they did not know Him, I gave them the Gospel. If they did not want to, I still asked for a donation for the church. Saved or not, I was asking for a donation for my Jesus to help spread the Gospel over the airwaves. Every now and then I would question myself about why I was doing this, for real.

This brings me back to the episode of Bozo Head, a.k.a. Leon.

After the six years of enjoying the Lord and the fellowship with the saints of God, the sin that I sinned was in my face. This is when I left and went home for two years without going to church anywhere. I was in a different apartment. Working and going to school. Just existing. I wished for a better existence. I was trying to find myself through different relationships *(is that what they call it now?)*, I got tired of that and just wanted to be left alone. A childhood friend showed up at my door. Didn't I just say that I wanted to be left alone? Well, she showed up at my door to tell me her brother is out of jail. My response in my head was, *So?* I smiled and said, "Oh good."

"He wants to come and see you."

"Okay."

He comes and never leaves. I married him.

This big idea popped in my head to go to church where I grew up. Remember I told you that I had made a vow never to step foot in another church, especially where the saints found no problem with lying about me? I forgave them though. (I'm smiling.) I kept telling myself back then, "I should tell them what really happened, I should tell them the truth." They were not ready to hear it; therefore, they kept believing the lie.

It felt so good to be there in the small but warm and inviting atmosphere. As is the custom in the Baptist church back then, the pastor went to the door and gave the benediction and stood there to shake the people's hands as they left the building. When it got to be my turn, I said to him, "Can I come back home?" Pastor hugged me, hugged me, hugged me! That was a yes.

Though I was now in a familiar place with people that I have known since childhood, and they knew me, there was still this agonizing, compelling piece to tell the other church what really happened and ask the question to why were you punishing me for a sin that was covered by the blood of Jesus and washed away by His Word? There is no such thing as forgive and forget. I believe we can honestly forgive, and as time goes by, the pain of the offense will go away as the Lord heals. But I had to make the choice to forgive. The forgetting part…well, the memory of the thing is there, but the pain associated with it will go away after the choice of forgiving takes its course.

Why did I feel it necessary to clear myself? One reason is because as a people pleaser, you want to look righteous in front of people. That ain't good. What am I to do about this?

I wrote a letter to the bishop and his first wife and held it because I wasn't sure about the response I would get. This was not a good time to have to deal with negative repercussions coming from a leader such as he. I held it. In the meantime, his wife passed away. I put the letter away. In the next year or so the matter was still stirring in my soul. I wrote another letter to the bishop and his new wife. I held it. In the meantime, he passed away. I asked the Lord why didn't I mail the letter, I needed answers, I wanted him to know the truth and no longer believe the lies. I received an answer in a dream. I'm telling you; God is so amazing! The dream was situated in a very large room at convocation time. Bishop was sitting with the other leadership on the platform. He spots me on the third row, comes down from the pulpit, and walks toward me. His face was filled with peace and the presence of God. I was smiling, but unsure about what was happening. When he got to where I was, there was an unspoken connection, an assurance that he knew what bothered me, that he knew the truth, and he was at peace and so was I. He walked back to his seat, and everything was perfect in the spirit. When I woke up, I could feel the peace and love of God all around me. The Lord, the King of Glory, had given me a blessed assurance that all is well, and forgiveness had done its work in me.

It was important to me that I had forgiven for real and that it wasn't just words. God does not play like that…

> But if ye do not forgive, neither will your
> Father which is in heaven forgive your trespasses.
> (Mark 11:26 KJV)

Sister, brother, if you ever find yourself in such a conundrum, seek the face of God, the God who sees you! I needed somebody to pray with me, to cry with me, to show me how to navigate through all of this stuff; this messy, messy stuff. The Holy Ghost was with me the whole time, otherwise the enemy of my soul could have easily taken me out because I was in agreement with him and out of alignment with God. What mercy the Lord has shown towards the rebelliousness of His children, towards me. He dealt with me according to His purpose for my life instead of my rebellion. This is when I learned the true value of what Jesus did for me on the cross. While I was yet sinning my sin, He gave His life for me. He paid the price for me to be free.

The Lord revealed His undying love for me when He did not put me away but reminded me that He is married to the backslider. Though my reactions to the things that had been done unjustifiably toward me were meant to destroy me, God did not allow it to be so. Are you asking why do I think it was unjustified? I thought I heard you ask that! Look at the timeline. I was not saved. Being unsaved does not make what I did right. It was as wrong and immoral as it could be. When I confessed the travesty that Bozo Head and I had created, it was nailed to the cross. This is how I knew that the Word of God is true. Read 2 Corinthians 5:15–19 (The Voice):

> He died for us so that we will all live, not for
> ourselves, but for Him who died and rose from
> the dead. Because of all that God has done, we
> now have a new perspective. We used to show
> regard for people based on worldly standards
> and interests. No longer. We used to think of the
> Anointed the same way. No longer. Therefore, if
> anyone is united with the Anointed One, that
> person is a new creation. The old life is gone—

and see—a new life has begun! All of this is a gift from our Creator God, who has pursued us and brought us into a restored and healthy relationship with Him through the Anointed. And He has given us the same mission, the ministry of reconciliation, to bring others back to Him. It is central to our good news that God was in the Anointed making things right between Himself and the world. This means He does not hold their sins against them. But it also means He charges us to proclaim the message that heals and restores our broken relationships with God and each other.

I asked this question of myself, and you could ask yourself as well, "What have I gotten from this ordeal, this turmoil, this way that seemed right but was leading to destruction?"

Read on for my answer…

CHAPTER 6

I Should Christian-Rap This Chapter!

The bishop is not God Jr.

Church is not God.

Ministry is not God.

God forgives, and that's it.

There are some Christians that will lie on purpose.

My response to negativity is my responsibility.

The devil can't make me do anything.

Don't be a people-pleasing saint. Instead please God.

Put no one on a pedestal.

Be sure that my anchor holds and grips the Solid Rock!

Work out my own soul salvation with fear and trembling!

God is always for me and never against me!

Honor God no matter what comes my way.

When I have to talk to someone, make sure it is a godly, trusted source.

I am anointed because God anointed me, not because I rubbed against an anointed brother or sister.

Trust God to work things out for my good.

There are people who love like Jesus. Discern who they are. Watch the fruit.

I am never alone in any trial.

I will be tested by God because He knows that I can pass the test. He trained me.

Don't live out of my past, learn from it, and share it to help another person.

I am not the only one.

Consider the sin I have committed against others, and ask for forgiveness.

Be quick to forgive. Hold nothing against anyone.

I am not holy without Jesus.

I am not Holy Ghost Jr.

God does not need my help, but He welcomes me to work alongside Him.

The Word of God judges all men.

If rejected, move on. You know…shake the dust off.

Steward relationships that the Lord has ordained.

Be kind and considerate. Courtesy is a hallmark of the Kingdom. (Thank you, Penelope.)

I am God's mouthpiece. I am a prophet of God.

People don't have to love me, but I absolutely must love them no matter what.

I don't need a bottle and a man to cope. I have new wine and the Holy Ghost.

Jesus is enough.

It is good to expose the devil and his antics against me and you.

Pride stinks. Be humble.

God is all about character.

It is possible to have the Holy Ghost and still backslide. It is a decision.

Be humble because pride has a stench to it.

Think and say about myself what God thinks
and says about who I am.
I have a whole lot to offer, so be myself in Christ.
I am not a carbon copy.
I am a treasured and honorable vessel.
Sometimes some folks are not part of the plan.
Let go of every weight that overwhelms and frus-
trates the plan of God in me.
The devil really does lie.
The flesh will always agree with the devil.
Do not backslide. It will confuse people.
If the devil's lips are moving, he's lying. Stop lis-
tening to the *vilelicity (vile-lisi-tee)*. Yes, I
made it up. He has vile and foul language
even when it sounds pretty.
My best friend will always be Jesus.
There are Christ-minded people who are trust-
worthy.
And those that are not.
All apostles, prophets, pastors, evangelists, and
teachers are not the same.
Time is short. Do what you are supposed to be
doing, and be done with it.
There could be consequences to your past sin.
There is always mercy.
Stop agreeing with the enemy of the soul. God
does not condemn His people.
Jesus is coming for sure.

CHAPTER 7

Finally

The takeaways I gained when church people and sinner people look the same to me are irreplaceable insight. I learned that everyone does not believe that the sinner that we were and the sin we committed before Christ is dead. Contrary to people's thoughts, our sins are just as dead as Jesus died on the cross on Calvary, nailed to the tree!

One more take away: *believe what Jesus did is sufficient.*

I'm not real sure if I should be thankful for Bozo Head leading me into bizarro world or very angry because he did. Nonetheless, even this has worked for God's glory and my good. God used all of that, and I mean every bit of it, to build me into the woman of God that I am. These kinds of things humble you—it did me. I have to be honest; it took a great deal of breaking to get to the humble part. Because of my path I became a mean person, and I did not want to be. This is what mean looked like in bizarro world: I chased my sister around the house with a butcher's knife. I called my sisters embarrassing names that to me were fitting, and I did it in front of their friends. Just mean and cantankerous. I didn't want to be that way. I was messed up inside, and no one knew how to help. Jesus did. That is why I am ever grateful to my mother who led me to Jesus. This is the greatest legacy she could have given. There were lots of questions inside that needed answers. I had to forgive a whole bunch of people. How do I forgive a dead man who molested me at five years old? Whenever my dad came to visit, I had to listen to him complain about my weight, so I made a point to put off seeing him as long as I could when he came to town. I forgave him for unkind words. As a matter of fact, he heard me preach a message at an 8:00 a.m. service and it was the last message he heard in the church. He came to the altar that Sunday. Not too long after that, he passed away.

You don't have to tell me what freedom feels like. I know bondage, and I know freedom from bondage. Anybody want to be free? Do yourself a favor. Forgive.

If there is a time to make sure there's nothing between me and what God has destined for my life…it was way past time! Forty-nine whole years! Forty-nine years is a mighty long time to withhold what should have been released at the time it was revealed.

Listen, there are innocent bystanders who were wounded by my silence. Just as some voices were loud against me, I was just as guilty by not correcting the ignorant lips by praying for them or by having that conversation with leadership. Do not leave this kind of thing up to chance. Pastors have a load to carry. When I thought that my leader should have known my character, he clearly did not; otherwise, it would have been nipped in the bud. I dread to think that another possibility is the obvious clique that was present. I am ever so grateful for peace and love.

Brother, sister, do you realize that the enemy of your soul wants to utterly destroy you? But he cannot unless you totally reject God's grace. Have you ever thought about reasons you are under attack, or why you make decisions that you *know* is going to lead to trouble? Why does it seem to be one thing after another in your life? Always, but always check your relationship with the Lord. Make sure it is in good standing. Check your heart for unforgiveness and disobedience. Repent. If these things are in order and all of the rigmarole is coming your way, *know this…your life is valuable to the kingdom and the body of Christ, and the devil is making every attempt to keep you from your assigned destiny. Good golly, man! He wants to destroy you and your bloodline!* Not so, though.

I would say to you, keep your heart clean and clear of debris. So when the Bozo Heads, the Susie Qs, and whatever they are dangling in front of you show up…*run, Forrest, run!*

Thank you for reading part of my life's story. I really would love to share other sections of it as the Lord leads me.

It is a bad feeling when you find out that you have judged someone based on a lie, isn't it? It's so unfair and unchristian, right?

This lie has now been exposed and corrected by the honest to goodness truth!

ABOUT THE AUTHOR

Carol Ann Blackwell, author of *Should I Tell Them the Truth Or Let Them Keep Believing a Lie?*, is a full-time lover of Christ, an anointed praise and worship leader, a prophet, a warrior, and a woman of wisdom. She also pastors alongside her husband, Pastor Darryl Blackwell of God's Way Ministries. She was born and raised in the beautiful state of Virginia and currently resides in North Carolina.

Writing is not new to Carol. She has also published volumes of poems and blogs dedicated to encouraging and equipping God's people for everyday living. Carol enjoys making natural care products that enhances the skin you are in.